Little Known Evidences of The Book of Mormon

(Adapted from a "Know Your Religion" lecture
given February 1988 in Scottsdale, Arizona)

by

Brenton G. Yorgason, Ph.D.

Dedicated to Paul Thomas Smith,
a dear friend who truly helped.

Brenton G. Yorgason
Little Known Evidences of The Book of Mormon

94 95 96 97 98 99 00 10 9 8 7 6 5 4
ISBN 1-55503-128-5

Books authored and/or coauthored by Dr. Blaine M. Yorgason

TY: The Ty Detmer Story
NAMINA—Biography of Georganna Bushman Spurlock (private printing)
Six Secrets of Self Renewal and Relationship Enhancement
The *First* Christmas Gift
Prayers on the Wind
Spiritual Survival in the Last Days
Here Stands a Man
Roger and Sybil Ferguson History (private printing)
Little Known Evidences of the Book of Mormon
Sacred Intimacy
Receiving Answers to Prayer
Obtaining the Blessings from Heaven
Dirty Socks and Shining Armor—A Tale from King Arthur's Camelot
Tales from the Book of Mormon
Pardners—Three Stories on Friendship
In Search of Steenie Bergman (Soderberg Series #5)
KING—A Biography of Jerome Palmer King (Private Printing)
The Greatest Quest
Seven Days for Ruby (Soderberg Series #4)
The Eleven Dollar Surgery
Becoming
The Loftier Way: Tales From the Ancient American Frontier
Brother Brigham's Gold (Soderberg Series #2)
Ride the Laughing Wind
The Miracle
The Thanksgiving Promise (paperback—movie version)
Chester I Love You (Soderberg Series #2)
Double Exposure
Seeker of the Gentle Heart
The Krystal Promise
A Town Called Charity, and Other Stories About Decisions
The Bishop's Horse Race (Soderberg Series #1)
Windwalker (movie version—out of print)
Others
From First Date to Chosen Mate
From Two to One
From This Day Forth (out of print)
Creating a Celestial Marriage (textbook)
Marriage And Family Stewardships (textbook)

Tapes authored and/or coauthored by Dr. Brenton G. Yorgason

Prayers on the Wind
Sacred Intimacy
Things Most Plain and Precious
The Joyous Way
Rhinestones and Rubies
The Miracle (dramatized tape of book)
The Bishop's Horse Race (taped reading of book)
Becoming (dramatized reading of book)
Chester I Love You (dramatized tape of book)
Little Known Evidences of the Book of Mormon

Part One

Not long ago, I began a journey that took me around the world to the mystical land of Saudi Arabia. It was a business trip, my second one to that part of the world; and the fact that I had been there before only whetted my appetite for what I would again see and feel.

I knew that I was going into Book of Mormon country, and because I wanted to drink deeply from the pages of that ancient journal while I was "on location," I took my eighty-four-year-old copy of the Book of Mormon from its shelf in my den, kissed my wife and children good-bye, and boarded the plane.

I began reading the title page of that weathered journal as my plane left Salt Lake International Airport, and I read continuously from there to London, and then on to Rome. Partaking of this visual feast was thrilling for me, especially since I was surrounded by seven newly-called missionaries who were on their way to Sicily to preach the same restored truths I was reading. While those missionaries labored to convert everyone on the plane, I just sat back and reminisced how my companions and I had done the same thing as we flew to the Florida mission some twenty-two years earlier.

I was halfway through the Book of Alma when we touched down in Saudi Arabia. Wishing to be uninterrupted while I read, I placed the book in my briefcase, and did not open it to read again until two weeks later as I left the sandy plains of Saudi Arabia. I then read nonstop, completing the final words of Moroni as the plane was taxiing into the JFK International Airport in New York City.

If one could ever want a baptism by fire or a consuming moment with the Holy Spirit, then spending nineteen hours in this manner is a singular way for that to transpire. Because I had learned the Semitic origins of many words and phrases in the Book of Mormon, and because I had taught its doctrinal principles for several years in seminary and at Brigham Young University, the timeliness of this feast couldn't have been more perfectly orchestrated.

Let me share one experience of that journey that puts my marathon reading experience in context.

As we flew into Saudi Arabia, we landed first in Jedda, having flown down past Egypt along the Red Sea that Moses parted one long-ago day. It was eerie to be flying over the same water wells or oases that Lehi, Nephi, and their family drank from as they were fleeing the soon-to-be-destroyed Jerusalem.

Leaving Jedda, we then flew to Riyadh, the capitol of this kingdom. As we traveled, our route took us directly over Mecca, the place where Mohammed taught words of wisdom to his people during the seventh century A.D. My stomach tightened as I remembered learning that only Muslims are allowed into this holy city of Mecca and that a non-Muslim would be immediately beheaded if he were to enter there.

We then flew on to Dhahran, on the eastern shore of the Persian Sea. We flew north of the desert section where Lehi's family nearly perished because there were no water holes until they reached their land Bountiful.

It was mind-boggling to me that a peninsula only one-third the size of the United States has several thousand acres of trees and wild beasts; it was truly a land of milk and honey. But that is the case, and today this small, fertile forest is part of a country called *Oman*. Little do the villagers of Oman realize that almost 2,600 years ago, a small, weary group entered this valley, built a ship under the direction of a young man likely in his early twenties, and then set sail for the land I have now inherited.

I don't know how a similar experience would have affected the testimony of others, but as I reread the account of Lehi's journey, while travelling in the luxury of a Boeing 747 over the very trail that he and his people walked during their eight-year journey to Oman, my heart filled to overflowing. I became consumed with love and admiration for these Earlier-day Saints because of the faith they had as they left the comforts of their homes in Jerusalem and departed along the Red Sea, their destination unknown to them at that time.

As I journeyed across that arid land, I recorded the following words in the fly-leaf of my aging Book of Mormon:

"We are truly a blessed people, and I bear solemn and reconfirmed testimony that I know the gospel of our Savior has been restored to this earth. The Book of Mormon is an authentic record of God's dealings with a very special family and their posterity. I am thankful that some of the members of this family were valiant in their charge to record their feelings, experiences, weaknesses, strengths, and especially their testimonies of Christ so that *my* family could progress in their own testimonies of necessity!"

I have thought often of President Ezra Taft Benson's counsel to drink from the pages of the Book of Mormon daily. I have found by my own experience that my thirst for those ancient writings continues to grow, and that I am more able to kneel in private morning prayer after I have pondered a few pages in this sacred journal. I truly know that, for me, reading the Book of Mormon gives greater power—not only in prayer but to resist wrong and adhere to right as I launch into my daily doings. Thus has been borne my desire to share with you the origins, as well as the clear, pure nourishment I have discovered in my delving into this unparalleled canon of scripture.

Even though my earliest memories of reading the Book of Mormon are of sitting among the members of my family in our living room while Dad read from its pages, my first personal encounter with the book took place in the summer preceding my senior year in high school, just after I had observed my seventeenth birthday.

The year was 1963, and I was spending the summer in Elko, Nevada, washing dishes at Slim Olsen's Cafe five miles west of town. With my extraordinary wage of $1.00 per hour and my room and board of only $1.00 per day, I was in financial heaven. Both because my room was in a small motel west of the cafe and because my roommate was a thirty-one-year-old divorced fellow, I felt quite safe and contented.

Although this environment provided me with a great learning experience as well as the money I needed to carry me through my senior year at Brigham Young High School in Provo, Utah, still it was not pure, and I was affected by it. I did manage to procure the graveyard shift, however, so I was almost always alone in my room to do what I pleased.

While living in those small quarters, I determined to find out for myself whether the Book of Mormon was true. Just a month before, my seminary teacher had admonished me to read the book that summer; so I set my jaw and determined to do just that.

I'll have to admit that reading that ancient record consumed many of my waking hours. It kept me away from any enticements of the gambling community, as well as from spending time with the wrong type of friends. Since I had promised my parents that I would maintain the level of righteousness they expected of me, this reading project became my shield and protection.

Even so, I read the book with a questioning mind. I realize now that even though my intentions were good, my spirit was impacted by the environment I had entered. I had made a decision to be morally clean, to live the Word of Wisdom, to refrain from using profanity, and to never participate in vulgar stories. Still, since I heard it all every night that I went to work, my mind was not totally pure as I visually consumed page after page of that book. Finally, with one hundred pages left to read, I determined that I would not sleep again until I had completed the book and had put Moroni's words (as found in Moroni 10:4-5) to the test.

And so, returning to my room at six o'clock one morning, I quickly showered and brushed my teeth. I then knelt in prayer, climbed into bed, and began one of the most significant days in my life.

Almost frantically I read each page, this time thinking that these wars and experiences, as well as the coming of Christ to America, really *could* have happened.

Finally, about twelve hours after I began, as the sun was setting to the west, I completed page 522 and closed the book. I then climbed quietly out of bed, knelt down, and began to pray. I felt that my prayers would be answered, as a matter of course, and that I could then arise and write my discovery to my parents back in Utah.

But to my astonishment and dismay, the more I prayed, the more darkness and spiritual abandonment I experienced. My mind could not comprehend what I was *feeling*, and yet I had a stupor of thought that lasted the entire hour that I spent on my knees.

Finally, exhausted and spent of tears, I concluded my prayer and climbed back into bed. I still had almost two hours until I had to be at work, so I just lay there, pondering the unexpected and totally unwanted feelings I had experienced.

I then arose, sat down at my small, make-shift desk, and wrote these words to my parents:

> Maybe I have done something that has displeased God. But I think I have truly repented of anything I might have done unknowingly. In other words, I'm just plain lost. I don't know where to turn to next. I have never felt this way before. However, I also know that it is my problem and that maybe I shouldn't cry on your shoulder because it is my problem. I just don't know.

I remember folding the letter over and putting it in the envelope, thinking, as I did, how alone and empty I felt. I sealed the envelope and climbed back in bed.

After spending a few moments in contemplation, I picked up my copy of the Book of Mormon, turned to page 520, and again read through Moroni's promise. He said that if I read the book "with a sincere heart, with real intent, having faith in Christ," that the truthfulness of it would be made manifest to me by the power of the Holy Ghost.

At that time, I made a tremendous, though painful, discovery. I had not read the first 400 pages either "with a sincere heart" or with "faith in Christ" that it *was* true. Though my mind had been contaminated with impure thoughts, caused largely by my environment, I expected everything of the Lord during my concluding hour of need. I then knew what I must do.

I arose, closed the book, and turned again to my knees. I then petitioned Father for forgiveness of any sins that I had committed and pledged to Him my commitment to keep all of the commandments so that I would be worthy to serve a mission in just twenty-two months.

At that moment, my spirit, body, and mind received the answer I was seeking. First, there was a surge of energy as I found myself engulfed in an unfamiliar blanket of warmth. Then there were tears of another nature as I felt a sense of forgiveness and peace that is still difficult for me to express and to share. I had my answer, clear and sweet to my soul, and so it was left to *me* to fulfill my side of the agreement.

I wish that I could say that I didn't sin again prior to my mission. I obviously can't say that, however, even though my desire was always to keep each commandment. Nor can I say now, twenty-seven years later, that I have completely eliminated transgression from my life; but I am doing better. Each year, as I have my temple recommend renewed, I prepare by making sure that during the past twelve months I have moved in the proper direction on that difficult and ofttimes steep ladder of purification.

And I have found, now that I have spent these years becoming more and more acquainted with the teachings of the Book of Mormon prophets and as I find application to my own life on each page, that my spirit is more refined and pure when I am reading that book than when I am not. This journey of discovery, together with applying my learning to the rearing of my nine children, has in fact become my greatest quest.

And so this brings me to the point of inquiry. Just *what* is *this book?* And what insights can we ponder that will assist us in understanding and then more closely attuning ourselves to a daily drink from its pages?

To answer these questions I would like to travel on two unique journeys into the past. While the second journey delves only into the last four decades, the first is a trek back into Church history to the time of Joseph's actual acquiring the golden record from the ancient American prophet, Moroni. Here we will set the stage for the bringing forth of this sacred, ancient journal by the twenty-one-year-old Joseph Smith.

Part Two

In traveling back to upstate New York in the early 1820's, we find ourselves surrounded by some fifty glacial deposits formed during the ice age. One of these, a long cigar-shaped glacial drumlin, was identified by the boy prophet, Joseph Smith. Before venturing into the mind and activities of young Joseph, perhaps it would be good to consider what was found in and around that hill some 200 years before the Smith family settled in that area.

Early historians recorded that the first settlers of this part of the state found the top soil white with a lime substance which comes from decayed human bones. In addition, the first farmers in this area plowed up thousands of arrowheads and spear points, which were scattered over the surface of the land. Many hills had been fortified with trees, some large and some short, which showed evidence of one time being felled and logged with sharp cutting tools. At Sandy Creek, a formidable fort was discovered. The trenches were eight to ten feet wide, and iron implements were excavated from them. The fort, itself, was in some way cut out of rock. Frontenac, who was an emissary to the King of France, made a report of these particulars, stating that it was very doubtful that the fort could have been built without the use of powder (*McCauley's History of New York*, 1828).

E.G. Squier, in his *Antiquities of New York* written in 1851, says of Cumorah-land: "Human bones of men, women, and children of both sexes, [and] of infant children, have been unearthed in long common trenches. The bodies were thrown together promiscuously by the thousands." This region of the country at one time possessed a very heavy Indian population. Pottery and pipes, flint arrowheads, stone hatchets, and other implements were found in great abundance. Squier further noted (pp. 137-38) that considerable evidence of Hebrew origins were found with the ancient relics, which, with his calculations, dated back at least several hundred years.

Josiah Priest, who authored *American Antiquities*, records: "We are far from believing the Indian of the present time to be the aborigines of America: but quite contrary, are usurpers who have by force of bloody warfare, exterminated the original inhabitants, taking possession of their country and property."

In addition to the above, many flint mines have been found in Cumorah-land. State Bulletin #2, New York says that several miles south of "Mormon Hill" another workshop was found where flint, arrowheads, spear points, and many unfinished weapons were found in abundance.

It was up those graceful slopes that Joseph Smith climbed to receive the gold plates from the prophet/historian, Moroni, who had buried them there approximately 1400 years earlier. At that time, the hill became known as "Mormon Hill," although Joseph later learned that it had been named *Cumorah* by Moroni; that was the name it was given by his people. Today, because of Joseph Smith, it is known throughout the world as—*Cumorah.*

It is now the predawn hours of September 22, 1827. Joseph and his new bride, Emma, have been married since the previous January 18th, and are at this hour returning from Joseph's ninth recorded visit with the angel, Moroni. These visits, spanning the previous four years, have given rise to an uncommon education for the youthful prophet.

When Joseph and Emma returned to their home, which was approximately two miles from the Hill Cumorah, the family was just serving breakfast. Joseph's mother, Lucy, had stayed up the entire night, waiting for her son to return with the ancient plates.

But Joseph did not bring the plates home with him. Instead, he ushered his mother into a room away from the family and visitors in the eating area. There he showed her the ancient interpreters. He said the angel had called them "Urim and Thummim," which means "light and perfection" in Hebrew. A friend and convert of a later time, Edward Stevenson stated that he had heard Lucy describe the Urim and Thummim as follows:

I found that the Urim and Thummim consisted of two smooth three-cornered diamonds, set in glass, and the glasses were set in silver bows, which were connected with each other in much the same way as old fashioned spectacles, only much larger. (*Reminiscences of the Prophet Joseph*, pp. 24, 27, 31.)

Several years later, in recording the events of that date, Joseph Knight, Sr., whose horse and carriage Joseph had borrowed to procure the plates, said the following:

He [Joseph Smith] had talked with me and told me the Conversation he had with the personage which told him if he would Do right according to the will of God he mite obtain [the sacred ancient plates] the 22nd Day of September Next and if not he never would have them. . . . So that night we all went to Bed and in the morning I got up and my Horse and Carriage was gone. But after a while he Came home and he turned out the Horse. All Come into the house to Brackfirst [breakfast]. But nothing said about where they had bin. After Brackfirst Joseph Cald me into the other room and he set his foot on the Bed and leaned his head on his hand and says, "Well I am Dissopinted." "Well," says I, "I am sorry." "Well," says he, "I am grateley Dissopinted; it is ten times Better than I expected." Then he went on to tell the length and width and thickness of the plates, and said he, "they appear to be Gold." But he seamed to think more of the glasses or the urim and thummem than he did of the Plates, for, says he, "I can see any thing; they are Marvelus" (Taken from Donna Hill's Joseph Smith, The First Mormon, pp. 70-71. In her footnote, Hill states that this statement by Knight is undated and unsigned, but was likely written between 1833 and 1847, the last of which is the year Knight died. The MS is in the Historical Department, Library/Archives Division.)

At the time he obtained the plates, Joseph explained to his mother that he had not brought them off the hill with him. Instead, he had carved out a section of bark from a fallen birch log and had placed the plates in the hollowed-out portion of the log. He then described how he had replaced the bark and had temporarily left the plates so that he could procure a box to put these plates in when he would finally bring them down off the hill.

According to Lucy, Joseph's mother, (*History of Joseph Smith*, pp. 103-106), Joseph then traveled some ten miles west of Palmyra to the small village of Macedon, where he was digging a well for

Mrs. Wells. His intent was to use the money earned to pay for the box that his brother, Hyrum, was having built to protect the plates.

Meanwhile, word leaked out that Joseph Smith had found some precious gold plates. Joseph's Father, Joseph Smith, Senior, had confided in a friend, Martin Harris. This was the same Martin Harris who had employed Joseph as a ten-year-old to work on his farm for fifty cents a day and who, in late 1826, had bought Joseph a new suit of clothes so that he could travel in style on his second journey to Harmony, Pennsylvania, and there make a good impression upon Emma and her father in order to ask for Emma's hand in marriage. But to continue with the story of obtaining the plates: Harris, in learning of Joseph's acquisition of the same, had shared the news with one Willard Chase, a Methodist class leader. Chase had seemingly hired a conjurer to come sixty or seventy miles to Palmyra and to *divine* where the plates were hidden.

It should be added, parenthetically, that Joseph had belonged to a group of fortune seekers that also included Willard Chase. The members of this group had evidently made a pact, or articles of agreement: that if any of their members found a buried treasure, it was his obligation to share the wealth of his find with the other members. Now, however, Joseph was not sharing his find. Rather, from their perspective, he was secretly hoarding it, keeping it from them. (*Joseph Smith, The First Mormon*, Donna Hill, p. 66.)

Joseph was brought back from Macedon by Emma, but upon gazing into the Urim and Thummim, he found the plates to be safe back on the hill. Nonetheless, he saddled his horse and, with his wife, went immediately back to his parents' home to obtain the sacred record.

Under the cloak of darkness, Joseph went again to the hill where the plates lay hidden. Unknown to him, however, three men had concealed themselves in various places in the nearby fields and were prepared to accost him as he returned from the hill with the plates. Even though they did attack him three times, he was able to flee their company.

Arriving back at his home, Joseph leaned up against the fence and only then realized that during one of the attacks he had dislocated his thumb. Joseph was undoubtedly beginning to understand the great effort Satan would exert to extract the plates from him.

Then, feeling that this group would continue to make attempts to obtain the plates, Joseph determined to hide the record until it could be safe. Thus, he took up the hearth-stone on one of the two fireplaces in his family's new home and buried the plates beneath the hearth. He had no sooner replaced the stone over the plates than Chase and his men forced themselves into the house.

With a divining rod, which was a large wishbone-shaped branch, these men divined that the plates were in the direct vicinity of the fireplace. For some reason, the group did not pursue this divined information, but strangely left the house at that time.

Again sensing that the plates were in danger, Joseph removed them from under the hearth and took them across the street to his father's cooper shop. Instead of putting the plates in the box that had been built for them, Joseph placed the gold record in the attic of the shop, wrapping them in flax. He then tore up the planks of the floor, deposited the empty box beneath it, and secured the planks in their former position.

Not long after Joseph returned to his home, Chase and his men, led by Chase's sister, Sally (who had a green stone that she purportedly could see things with), showed up at the cooper shop. They tore up the planks and smashed the box, but to no avail. Again the plates were protected.

Nor did Willard Chase, his sister, Sally, and the others give up. Realizing that they would have great difficulty translating the record while living in the Smith home, Joseph and Emma determined to go back to Harmony, Pennsylvania (where Emma was from) and translate there, hopefully in peace. Joseph had traveled down to Emma's home a few weeks earlier and had made amends with her parents for having married their daughter without their permission. They felt anxious to move there and live without persecution while Joseph translated the plates.

Arriving safely in Harmony, Joseph began immediately to translate what was to be known as the Book of Lehi. Emma was his chief scribe at this time, although Reuben Hale, Emma's brother, assisted as scribe during part of this early translation period. Martin Harris also arrived from Palmyra to assist and was soon sent to New York to Professor Charles Anthon to verify the translation of the ancient hieroglyphics.

After returning from New York, Martin persisted in trying to persuade Joseph to allow him to take the completed Book of Lehi, which consisted of 116 pages, to show his wife and other family members. After being denied permission twice by the Lord by looking into the Urim and Thummim, Joseph was finally given permission for Martin to take them and to show them to his wife, his father and mother, and to a Mrs. Cobb, a sister of his wife. (*History of the Church,* Vol. 1, p. 21.)

In his excitement Martin forgot his promise, the result of which was the loss of these early pages. This was a very painful moment for Joseph: he knew that he had erred in allowing the pages out of his possession. He then had another visit with Moroni and was severely reprimanded. Moroni took the plates and the interpreters from Joseph and left the youthful prophet a lonely, humbled man through that summer of 1828.

Finally, on the 22nd of September, the anniversary of his first receiving the plates a year earlier, Joseph again received the plates from Moroni. For an unknown reason, the plates were once more retrieved by Moroni, but for only a brief time.

Upon Moroni's second return of the plates to Joseph, additional revelations were received between September of 1828 and June of 1829. Today, these revelations are found in the Doctrine and Covenants, Sections 5, 6, 8, 9, 10, 17, all of which pertain to the Book of Mormon and its witnesses.

Joseph continued to study the plates through that winter, without doing any serious translating. From his eventual mastery of that ancient language, it is likely that he studied the ancient characters and reacquainted himself with the language of the first 116 pages that had been lost. He had no one to assist him, so the task of translation lay dormant through those winter months.

Finally, after a lengthy wait, Joseph was ready to proceed with the full thrust of translating the plates. In his words:

> On the 5th day of April, 1829, Oliver Cowdery came to my house, until which time I had never seen him. He stated to me that having been teaching school in the neighborhood where my father resided, and my father being one of those who [was] sent to the school, he went to board for a season at his house, and while there the family related to him the circumstance of my having received

the plates, and accordingly, he had come to make inquiries of me. Two days after the arrival of Mr. Cowdery (being the 7th of April) I commenced to translate the Book of Mormon, and he began to write for me, which having continued for some time, I inquired of the Lord through the Urim and Thummim, and obtained. (Section 6 of the Doctrine and Covenants.)

During the month of April I continued to translate, and he to write, with little cessation, during which time we received several revelations. (*History of the Church*, pp. 31-32.)

Through the process of translating of initial 116 pages, Joseph learned the ancient reformed Egyptian language.

In addition to becoming acquainted with Lehi and his family and culture, the translation of the 116 pages may have included the purpose of Joseph learning and mastering that ancient language. From my perspective, this is why the Lord had him do it. He had to go to school. Sometime before receiving the golden plates, an unusual event occurred. One day, while earning some money by digging a well for a man, Joseph found a large, chocolate-colored, egg-shaped stone. It was somewhat flattened, and he was told by the Lord to use this stone as a "seer stone." (*Millennial Star*, Martin Harris' statement, vol XLIV, p. 87). This seer stone played a major role years later during the translating of the plates.

There were times during the translating that Joseph chose not to strap on the breastplate—a large, metal *structure* that was fastened, according to Joseph's mother, by four metal-like straps. She indicated that these four straps were two finger-widths wide and that two of them fit over the shoulders while the other two fit around the wearer's waist. (*History of Joseph Smith*, p. 111). The Urim and Thummim, which appeared to be similar to a large pair of spectacles, was then attached to the breastplate by a rod inserted into the upper right corner of the breastplate so that Joseph could translate with his hands free.

The seer stone that Joseph had found several years earlier now becomes relevant to the translation process. When Joseph chose not to use the Urim and Thummim, he would simply place this seer stone into a hat. He would then prepare himself spiritually to translate and would then gaze into the hat. The stone would light up and he would use the instrument as directed. David Whitmer states the following:

In the darkness the spiritual light would shine. A piece of something resembling parchment would appear, and under it was the interpretation in English. Brother Joseph would read off the English to Oliver Cowdery, who was his principal scribe, and when it was written down and repeated to brother Joseph to see if it was correct, then it would disappear and another character with the interpretation would appear. (Address to All Believers in Christ, a pamphlet published by David Whitmer, 1887, p. 12.) Joseph also used the seer stone to receive information pertaining to the kingdom, to warn him of danger, etc., just as he used the Urim and Thummim. In fact, he began to use the terms "seer stone" and "Urim and Thummim" interchangeably.

Joseph stated that it was not for us to know all of the details of the translating of the plates. He did say enough to give us clues such as that described above during the translating of the first 116 pages.

David Whitmer said that he helped as scribe whenever Oliver tired of writing. This assistance was likely after Joseph and Emma moved 110 miles north to the Peter Whitmer, Senior farm to complete their translation.

As another illustration of how the seer stone was used during the translation of the plates, there was an occasion, early on, when Martin Harris was helping. He and Joseph determined to take a rest, so they left the home and went down to the creek to skip stones. While there, Martin found a stone that closely resembled the seer stone that he knew was in the hat upstairs in the house.

Without saying anything to Joseph, Martin took the stone into the house, exchanged it for the seer stone, and then waited for Joseph to return so they could resume their translating.

Joseph soon entered the room, sat down and readied himself for the continuation of their work. After gazing for a few moments into the hat, he exclaimed, "Martin, what is the matter? All is as dark as Egypt; I cannot read a thing!" (*Millennial Star* 44:78-79, 86-87.)

Martin responded by giving back the correct stone to Joseph and indicated rather sheepishly that he had tested Joseph simply to stop the mouths of fools—fools who had told him that Joseph had merely learned the sentences and was simply repeating them.

Referring to the process of translating the plates, we see from early statements that the process was likely an evolving one. Dr. Paul Cheesman in his book, *The Keystone of Mormonism* (pp. 40-51), provides a lengthy discussion and series of statements made by those associating with Joseph during this early hour of his being a prophet/translator. In addition, Elder Mark E. Peterson (*Those Gold Plates*, pp. 47-64) describes the early conditions and procedures in translating the plates. As far as we know, Joseph made no specific references to the method of translating other than what is recorded in D&C 9:7-9. In the record of a meeting of priesthood brethren in Ohio, we also find the following:

> Brother Hyrum Smith said that he thought best that the information of the coming forth of the Book of Mormon be related by Joseph himself to the Elders present, that all might know for themselves.
>
> Brother Joseph Smith, Jun., said that it was not intended to tell the world all the particulars of the coming forth of the Book of Mormon; and also said that it was not expedient for him to relate these things. (*History of the Church*, 1:220.)

Perhaps one statement by Edward Stevenson, who reported Martin Harris' explanation of the method of translation, would be insightful as well as appropriate to share:

> Martin explained the translation as follows: By aid of the seer stone, sentences would appear and were read by the prophet and written by Martin, and when finished he would say, "Written," and if correctly written, that sentences would disappear and another appear in its place, but if not written correctly it remained until corrected, so that the translation was just as it was engraven on the plates, precisely in the language then used. (*Millennial Star*, 44:78-79.)

Whatever the exact manner of translation, we do know that the process required total worthiness on the part of Joseph. We also know that he became so conversant in the language and culture of the ancient Nephite people, that he did not even need the plates toward the end of the translation. He used either the Urim and Thummim or the seer stone through the entire procedure. But there were times when he did not use the *plates* while translating; these portions of the record may well have been received by direct revelation. (David Whitmer, *Kansas City Journal*, June 5, 1881.)

In sum, then, it would appear that the translation of the ancient plates was a result of Joseph's serious study of the ancient people and their language. Also, the translation was made possible by a special gift of translation provided by the Lord to this young seer.

The actual time Joseph spent in translating the plates is perhaps one of the most remarkable achievements of Joseph's life. Mark E. Peterson (*Those Gold Plates*, p. 51) states that Joseph translated the entire book "in about forty-five working days." In the February 1986 newsletter of the Foundation for Ancient Research and Mormon Studies, we have an even more precise statement:

> Among the amazing facts about the Book of Mormon is the astonishingly short time Joseph took to translate it. Recent research into the historical record shows it unlikely that any more than 65 to 75 days were involved in the actual translation.
>
> Translation of the Book of Mormon, as we have it today, did not begin in earnest until April 7, 1829, after the arrival of Oliver Cowdery in Harmony, Pennsylvania. Before this time, Joseph had translated only the 116 pages of the Book of Lehi (which transcript Martin Harris lost) and had worked on a few pages with Emma as his scribe. Working "with little cessation," Joseph and Oliver had reached 3 Nephi 11 by May 15, and they apparently completed the Plates of Mormon by May 31. This appears likely, since the Title Page at the end of these plates was translated before June 11, the date on which the full text of the Title Page appears in the copyright application for the Book of Mormon. At that point, no more than 55 days had transpired.
>
> The work continued after a move to the Whitmer farm in Fayette, New York. It appears that the Small Plates of Nephi were translated at this time. By mid-June, Joseph and Oliver had finished 1 Nephi and had reached 2 Nephi 27, which most likely sparked the manifestation to the Three Witnesses. Thus, about 20 days in June.
>
> Total days: Hardly more than 75. Probably less. These were busy days. From April to June, one must also allow Joseph time to reveal sections of the D&C; to restore the Priesthood; to baptize others; to give personal instructions to Oliver, Hyrum and Samuel Smith, and Joseph Knight; to move on buckboard from Harmony to Fayette (3 to 4 days); to obtain the copyright; and to eat and sleep.
>
> In practical terms alone, this is an impressive feat: 7 to 10 current book pages per day, final copy, day after day. Imagine on average, only a day and a half to compose King Benjamin's speech, or a week to do 1 Nephi, or a couple of hours for Alma 26! No wonder Oliver wrote in 1834, "These days were never to be forgotten." (*Times and Seasons*, 2:201.)

It would not be fair to pass by a statement made by Emma, Joseph's wife, just prior to her death in 1879. She was being interviewed by her son, Joseph Smith III, as reported in *The Saints Advocate*, October 1879:

> My belief is that the Book of Mormon is of divine authenticity—I have not the slightest doubt of it. I am satisfied that no man could have dictated the writing of the manuscript unless he was inspired; for when (I was acting) as scribe, your father would dictate to me hour after hour; and when returning after meals, or after interruptions, he would at once begin where he had left off, without either seeing the manuscript or having any portion of it read to him. It would have been improbable that a learned man could do this; and for one so . . . unlearned as he was, it was simply impossible.
>
> Joseph Smith could neither write nor dictate a coherent and well worded letter, let alone dictating a book like the Book of Mormon, and though I was an active participant in the scenes that transpired, and was present during the translating of the plates, and had cognizance of things as they transpired, it is marvelous to me, "a marvel and a wonder," as much so as to anyone else.

At the conclusion of the translation period, we have seven secondary statements that describe Joseph and his associates going up into a room within the Hill Cumorah, and there depositing the plates. (See "A Preliminary Draft of the Hill Cumorah Cave Story Utilizing Seven Secondary Accounts and Other Historical Witnesses" by Paul T. Smith, March 1980.)

Perhaps what should be shared at this time is a statement that President Brigham Young made while speaking at a special conference in Farmington, Utah, in 1877 just prior to his death. The purpose of the conference was to organize a stake of Zion for the county of Davis on that Sunday afternoon, June 17th. He states:

> I lived right in the country where the plates were found from which the Book of Mormon was translated, and I know a great many things pertaining to that country.

(Actually, a youthful Brigham Young was only ten miles away from Palmyra, in Mendon, when Joseph brought the plates down from the hill. In fact, he later stated that he heard a man named Walters talk of the great dollar value of the plates that this young

Joseph Smith had supposedly unearthed. It was more than four years later that Brigham read his brother-in-law's newly printed copy of the Book of Mormon and thereby gained a testimony of its validity.)

I believe I will take the liberty to tell you of another circumstance that will be as marvelous as anything can be. This is an incident in the life of Oliver Cowdery, but he did not take the liberty of telling such things in meeting as I take. I tell these things to you, and I have a motive for doing so. I want to carry them to the ears of my brethren and sisters, and to the children also, that they may grow to an understanding of some things that seem to be entirely hidden from the human family.

Oliver Cowdery went with the Prophet Joseph when he deposited these plates. Joseph did not translate all of the plates; there was a portion of them sealed, which you can learn from the book of Doctrine and Covenants. When Joseph got the plates, the angel instructed him to carry them back to the hill Cumorah, which he did. Oliver says that when Joseph and Oliver went there, the hill opened, and they walked into a cave, in which there was a large and spacious room. He says he did not think, at the time, whether they had the light of the sun or artificial light; but that it was just as light as day. They laid the plates on a table; it was a large table that stood in the room. Under this table there was a pile of plates as much as two feet high, and there were altogether in this room more plates than probably many wagon loads; they were piled up in the corners and along the walls.

The first time they went there the sword of Laban hung upon the wall; but when they went again it had been taken down and laid upon the table across the gold plates; it was unsheathed, and on it was written these words: "This sword will never be sheathed again until the kingdoms of this world become the kingdom of our God and his Christ."

I tell you this as coming not only from Oliver Cowdery, but others who were familiar with it, and who understood it just as well as we understand coming to this meeting, enjoying the day, and by and by we separate and go away, forgetting most of what is said, but remembering some things. So it is with other circumstances of life. I relate this to you, and I want you to understand it. I take this liberty of referring to those things so that they will not be forgotten and lost. Carlos Smith was a young man of as much veracity as any young man we had, and he was a witness to these things. Samuel Smith saw some things, Hyrum saw a good many things, But Joseph was the leader. (*Journal of Discourses*, 19:37-39.)

From Paul Smith's research of the other six accounts of this depository, we learn that sometime after the first of July, 1829, these men returned the plates to this cave. They could not take the plates back to the stone box from which it had first emerged, as this box had been discovered by local residents who later dug it out. According to these accounts, the room was presided over by a heavenly messenger, possibly Moroni.

We also learn from these accounts that some time later (possibly after the publication of the Book of Mormon in March of the following year), Joseph and Oliver again went to this cave. If later accounts may be believed, Joseph may have taken other members of Joseph's family with them, namely his father, Joseph, Senior, and his brothers, Hyrum, Don Carlos, and Samuel Harrison.

Of these men who accompanied Joseph, Oliver had been one of the original Three Witnesses to seeing the plates at the feet of Moroni, and all but Don Carlos were part of the group of eight witnesses who saw and handled the plates the previous year. One can imagine the joy Joseph felt as he had been given permission to share this singular event with his father and brothers!

Many unusual experiences took place during the translating period. In considering just who actually saw the plates during this time, we have record that Joseph's parents, Lucy and Joseph, Senior, felt them through a pillow case, although they never actually saw them (even though Joseph, Senior would later view them as one of the Eight Witnesses). In addition, a man by the name of Joshua McCune indicated that he felt and lifted the metal record through a pillow case, although Joseph didn't actually allow him to see the plates.

Emma never stated that she saw the plates, although she repeatedly attested to their presence in her home. She frequently moved the covered plates while cleaning the table and later remarked that they made a metallic clinking sound as they were moved. Emma died in 1879, and even on her deathbed, she did not declare having seen the plates. But she did indicate that Joseph always kept the ancient record covered and protected. It must have been interesting to learn of Emma's integrity, as the wife of the youthful seer, to never doubt their existence. The gold plates, if they had been made of pure gold, would have weighed approximately

200 pounds. If this was their substance, they would have been very soft and easily bent. If, however, the plates had been fashioned of gold with a copper alloy (thus making them much harder and more durable and lasting), they would have weighed fifty to sixty pounds, being six to eight carat gold.

Franklin S. Harris, Jr., conducted a study which he titled, "Old World Writing on Metal Plates." From his report, we learn that there have actually been sixty-two different sets of plates unearthed since the time that the gold plates came out of the Hill Cumorah. Of these sixty-two, nineteen were classified as gold, even though some had a type of alloy in them. The rest were classified as either silver, copper, or bronze. Many of these were unearthed in large stone boxes that had been cemented together in much the same way that Joseph described the stone depository which held the gold plates.

In referring again to the nature and use of the Urim and Thummim, we learn that Joseph was not the first prophet to be granted this aid in his stewardship. In fact, there are six different Biblical references and four Book of Mormon references of prophets using this instrument. Whether the instrument was the exact one given to Joseph, or another, we are not told.

Joseph indicated that the Urim and Thummim he had was the very same instrument used by the Brother of Jared when he was instructed by the Lord how he should build his ships (Ether 3:24; D&C 17:1). Also, Ammon, in the Book of Mormon, states that Mosiah had these instruments (Mosiah 8:13), and that a person possessing this instrument "can look, and translate all records that are of ancient date." Ammon also states that a person who is given the charge of translating must be commanded of God to perform this task and that such a man is called a "seer."

In Abraham 3:1-4 of the Pearl of Great Price, we are told that father Abraham used a Urim and Thummim to gain his knowledge of astronomy. We are also instructed in the Old Testament that Moses used a Urim and Thummim in learning how to use his priesthood in leading the children of Israel out of Egypt (Exodus 28:30; Leviticus 8:8; Numbers 27:21). Orson Pratt relates in great detail the use of these instruments by Moses and his brother, Aaron, as well as the use of the breastplate (*Journal of Discourses*, 18:156). In addition, Orson Pratt states that Noah used a similar instrument in fashioning his ark before the great flood (*Journal of Discourses*, 16:50). Also, Mosiah tells us (Mosiah 28:14) that the Urim and Thummim "were prepared from the beginning, and were handed down from generation to generation, for the purpose of interpreting languages."

Several LDS scholars maintain that the first portion of the Book of Mormon was translated through the use of the Urim and Thummim, but that it was completed by means of a seer stone. All other references to a Urim and Thummim seem to be generally used to mean a "seer stone."

The Urim and Thummim used by Joseph Smith may or may not have been given back to Moroni with the plates at the conclusion of the translation. We know from the statement that follows that Wilford Woodruff stated that Joseph showed him the Urim and Thummim on December 27th, 1841 (Wilford Woodruff Journal, Dec. 27, 1841).

> The twelve, or part of them, spent the day with Joseph the Seer, and he confided unto them many glorious things of the Kingdom of God. . . . I had the privilege of seeing for the first time in my day, the Urim and Thummim.

Now, this instrument shown to Brother Woodruff may have been the seer stone and not the actual ancient spectacles. We don't know. We do know, though, that an event transpired in the July preceding Joseph's death that implies that Joseph used the ancient instrument at that time. In *Comprehensive History of the Church* (2:106), we learn that in discussing the revelation received on plural marriage, it is recorded that

> He [Hyrum] then requested Joseph to write the revelation by means of the Urim and Thummim, but Joseph in reply said he did not need to, for he knew the revelation perfectly from beginning to end.

We also learn from Orson Pratt that Joseph used this ancient instrument in translating the Book of Abraham, which writings were found with the Egyptian mummies acquired from one Michael Chandler.

> The Prophet translated the part of these writings which, as I have said is contained in the Pearl of Great Price, and known as the

Book of Abraham. Thus you see one of the first gifts bestowed by the Lord for the benefit of His people, was that of revelation—the gift to translate, by the aid of the Urim and Thummim, the gift of bringing to light old and ancient records. (*Journal of Discourses*, 20:65.)

In addition to the use of the Urim and Thummim by Joseph, years later Heber C. Kimball stated that Brigham Young used this ancient instrument.

Has Brother Brigham Young got the Urim and Thummim? Yes, he has got everything. . .that is necessary for him to receive the will and mind of God to this people. Do I know it? Yes, I know all about it. (*Journal of Discourses*, 2:111.)

Regarding the seer stone itself, we know that it was given to Oliver Cowdery, who died in March of 1850. His widow later gave it to Phineas Young, who in turn gave it to his brother, Brigham. It is, of course, in possession of the Church today and to my knowledge was last displayed in public during the dedication of the Manti Temple. At that time, President Wilford Woodruff placed it on the altar of the temple as he offered the dedicatory prayer.

During the twenty-four years following the First Vision, it has been documented that Joseph Smith visited and communicated with many individuals from the spirit world. That must have been an enlightened condition for Joseph to live in. He was indeed a spiritual *amphibian*, living with one foot on each side of the veil, spending a great deal of time with prophets who lived hundreds of years earlier.

Of these, we know that in addition to Moroni's many visits, Joseph also had several interviews with the prophet, Nephi, with Mormon and his son, Moroni, and with others, including Alma. (*Journal of Discourses*, 13:47; 17:37; 23:362.)

From other records, we also know that Joseph visited with Adam, Moses, Elijah, John the Baptist, Peter, James, and John, as well as the Three Nephites.

Before leaving this time period, and the moment of Joseph's learning to receive revelation and to use "interpreters," I would like to explore a final thought. In D&C 130:8-11, a revelation Joseph Smith received on April 2nd, 1843, while at Ramus, Illinois, we learn the following:

The place where God resides is a great Urim and Thummim.
This earth, in its sanctified and immortal state, will be made like

unto crystal and will be a Urim and Thummim to the inhabitants who dwell thereon, whereby all things pertaining to an inferior kingdom, or all kingdoms of a lower order, will be manifest to those who dwell on it; and this earth will be Christ's.

Then the white stone mentioned in Revelation 2:17, will become a Urim and Thummim to each individual who receives one, whereby things pertaining to a higher order of kingdoms will be made known;

And a white stone is given to each of those who come unto the celestial kingdom, whereon is a new name written, which no man knoweth save he that receiveth it. The new name is the key word.

From what Joseph received on this date and from what John the Beloved mentions in Revelation, those who inherit the celestial kingdom will become seers in their own right. It behooves us, then, to put our lives in order, to purify our own vessels, and to make ourselves ready for this unique and unparalleled opportunity and blessing.

After completing the above research, I discovered a new and even more exhaustive account of Joseph Smith's early experiences, including details surrounding the translation of the sacred plates. This account is by Dr. Paul R. Cheesman and is titled the *Keystone of Mormonism—Early Visions of the Prophet Joseph Smith*, Eagle Systems International, 1988. While I have not drawn upon Dr. Cheesman's research, I highly recommend the reading of this treatise.

Part Three

Now for the second journey that I promised—an intellectual, yet a faith-promoting jaunt. I would like to bring you forward in time to our own day and focus on several events that transpired on the campus of Brigham Young University in Provo, Utah. From this springboard I would like to then travel with you north to the University of Utah in Salt Lake City and discuss an experience that, in context, sheds great light on the authenticity of the Book of Mormon.

The first event took place in 1958. At this time, a seminary teacher by the name of Glade L. Burgon published a thesis that centered on the question of whether one or more styles of writing was used in the Book of Mormon (Burgon, Glade L., "An Analysis of Style Variation in the Book of Mormon," Brigham Young University, Provo, Utah, 1958). He examined the writing styles of the four central Book of Mormon prophets—Nephi, Jacob, Mormon, and Moroni—and found four distinct styles of writing, as summarized below.

> Nephi: He used long sentences made of several dependent clauses. In his writing, metaphors were numerous and original, such as 'thunderings and lightnings of his power' (1 Nephi 19:11). He also used many personifications, such as 'they (other churches) will be drunken with their own blood' (1 Nephi 22:13). Nephi also used dialogue two to five times more frequently than did the other writers.

> Jacob: He used shorter, clearer sentences with less subordination. He also used many elliptical expressions. Apostrophe (speaking to

an unseen audience) was entirely absent. In addition, he used few parallels, and no redundant repetition other than a characteristic use of subject-participial phrase-subject (repeated).

Mormon: His writing are replete with infinitives. He used no ellipticals in contrast with Jacob's writings. He had an abundant use of Apostrophe, and of course dialogue in his writings is entirely absent. In addition, he exuded little use of the rhetorical question so frequently found in the writings of Moroni, his son.

Moroni: His use of participial phrases were half as numerous as in the other writings. He had a habit of using antithetical parallelisms (see Mormon 8:37), and used the Apostrophe with abundance. Moroni's writings were also characterized by an abundant amount of reasoning and use of the rhetorical question.

A decade and a half later, a group of researchers in the Statistics Department at BYU determined to broaden an examination of the twenty-four major authors of the Book of Mormon. (Larsen, Wayne A., Rencher, Alvin C., & Layton, Tim, "Multiple Authorship in the Book of Mormon," *New Era*, November, 1979, pp. 10-13.)

The objective of this group was to statistically compare the writing styles of these early journal keepers to those of Joseph Smith and his contemporaries (including that of Solomon Spaulding, an early 19th-century writer who died in 1830), as well as to compare the words spoken by Christ, as found in both the New Testament and Third Nephi in the Book of Mormon.

Their findings referred to in this discussion were enlarged upon in *BYU Studies*, Spring 1980. Basically, through studying the frequency of specific word usage (which developed into personalized "wordprints" much like our modern individualized "fingerprints"), they found it highly probable that the writings of many different authors exist in the Book of Mormon. They also examined writings of Joseph Smith, W.W. Phelps, Oliver Cowdery, Parley P. Pratt, Sidney Rigdon, and Solomon Spaulding. They found that none of the wordprints of the modern authors resembled the Book of Mormon wordprints. In their summary, they state the following:

> All of our data point to one almost inescapable conclusion: No one man wrote the Book of Mormon. It seems impossible that Joseph Smith or any other writer, however brilliant, could have

fabricated a work with 24 or more discernible wordprints. Especially when the 24 authors do not appear in 24 separate blocks, but are shuffled and intermixed in the most complicated manner imaginable. How could anyone keep track of so many word frequencies so as to vary them, not only randomly from one section to another, but also according to a fixed, underlying pattern? And remember, the whole concept of a non-contextual wordprint was unknown in Joseph Smith's day.

In short, while our analysis may not prove that the Book of Mormon was written by ancient Americans, it certainly seems to disprove most of the theories advanced by its opponents. (p. 13.)

Nearly a decade later, Dr. John L. Hilton joined forces with a group of non-LDS scholars, who called themselves the Berkeley Group. The purpose of their research was to study the author authenticity of the Book of Mormon. Taking a different approach than the earlier BYU Group, these researchers measured "word patterns" in the Book of Mormon. In his paper "Some Book of Mormon 'Wordprint' Measurements Using 'Wraparound' Block Counting" (published in Foundation for Ancient Research and Mormon Studies, July, 1988), Hilton and his colleagues (who, by the way, consisted of men of varied philosophic backgrounds, such as agnostic, Jewish, etc.) examined the texts of Nephi and Alma in the Book of Mormon. They then compared the "stylometry" or wordprints they found in those two books with those of Joseph Smith, Oliver Cowdery, and Solomon Spaulding.

In essence, these scholars found an extremely low probability that any of the above mentioned contemporaries authored the writings of Nephi and Alma. They also found that the books of Nephi and Alma were, in fact, written by different authors. They state the following:

> The proposition that Joseph Smith or Oliver Cowdery or Solomon Spaulding was the author of the Book of Mormon didactic writings of Nephi or Alma is statistically indefensible. The writings of Nephi and Alma are statistically independent of each other, much as are the writings of our independent non-contested control authors. However, the rate at which new words are introduced in the Book of Mormon texts consistently measures a low single value throughout the whole book. A simple (if not the simplest) consistent explanation for these two objectively measured

phenomena is that the Book of Mormon is a continuous literal translation of non-English writings by different original authors, expressed by a literal translator using a restricted English vocabulary. (p. 12.)

Let us now consider two final studies. A man by the name of William A. Kurz has researched twenty-two farewell addresses from classical and Semitic leaders of the past. As summarized in *Foundation for Ancient Research and Mormon Studies* (FARMS), June 1987, Kurz discloses twenty semitic criteria for a farewell speech. All but one of the twenty are found in King Benjamin's farewell address.

The following summary of these criteria are a bit cumbersome, but provide those of us of a Western mind a glimpse into the totally Near Eastern nature of this sermon:

Kurz' Criteria	Reference in Mosiah
1. The speaker summons successors	1:9-10; 2:1, 9
2. His own mission is an example	2:12-14, 18
3. His innocence; fulfilled his duty	2:15, 27-31
4. His impending death	1:9; 2:26, 28
5. He exhorts his audience	2:9, 40-41; 4:9-10; 5:12
6. Warnings/final injunctions	2:31-32, 36-39; 3:12, 25; 4:14-30; 5:10-11
7. He blesses his audience	Not clearly found, but see "blessed" in 2:41
8. Farewell gestures	Implied in 2:28; see 2 Ne 9:44
9. Tasks for successors	1:15, 16; 2:31; 6:3
10. Theological review of history	2:34-35; 3:13-15
11. Speaker reveals future	3:1, 5-10
12. Promises are given	2:22, 31; 4:12; 5:9
13. Appoints/refers to successor	1:15-16; 2:31; 6:3
14. The rest bewail loss of the leader	Not found
15. Future degeneration addressed	3:23-27; 4:14-15

16. Sacrifices and covenant renewal	2:3; 5:1-7
17. Care of those left	4:14-26; 6:3
18. Consolation to inner circle	5:15
19. Didactic (preachy) speech	3:16-21
20. *Ars moriendi*	Possibly in 2:28

In further support of King Benjamin's Israelite farewell sermon, John W. Welch, another LDS Semitic scholar, states in the same FARMS Update, "[it is] the fullest and the most complete example of this ancient speech typology anywhere in world literature."

Dr. Roger R. Keller conducted additional research by comparing the writing techniques of Mormon and Moroni as both authors and abridgers (*FARMS Update, April 1988*). As quoted in this report, Keller's initial findings indicate the following:

1. When Mormon is acting as an abridger, he interacts extensively with the underlying documents he is abridging. It is usually possible (although not always) to distinguish Mormon's own words and comments from the words that he draws from the materials he is condensing. As one reads along in many sections of the Book of Mormon abridged by Mormon, one often senses that a subtle shift has taken place as a smooth, almost imperceptible transition occurs from the underlying historical narrative to Mormon's commentary on that narrative. By carefully backtracking, one can discern, however, where the transition was made.

Moroni, on the other hand, interacts far less extensively with the text he is abridging. Moroni is usually careful about marking the beginning and ending of the comments that he has inserted into the abridged record.

This [observation] seems to indicate that Moroni was far less aggressive than Mormon as an abridger, perhaps because Moroni's task was limited to completing the record of his father. Thus, he may have felt less liberty than Mormon in molding, shaping, and interacting with the text he was editing.

2. A thorough statistical examination of vocabulary gives considerable evidence that each author is distinguishable. For example, the widely spaced sections of Mormon's own writings

manifest affinity for certain words, such as *baptism, hope, love,* and *wickedness.* On the other hand, the disparate writings of Moroni have another set of prevalent words in common, including *blood, destruction, suffer, faith, miracles,* and *power.* Furthermore, the vocabulary of the record of Ether [which record Moroni abridges] differs noticeably from all other portions of the Book of Mormon.

3. Furthermore, if one examines the words that are of importance to Mormon or to Moroni, when writing themselves, and then examines the relative frequency of these words in abridged portions of their records, some interesting observations can be made. Words prevalent in the writings of Mormon himself are usually of less importance in the edited texts. However, should a word important to Mormon appear in the underlying materials, this tends to increase Mormon's usage of that word as he comments on the matter, especially in the books of Mosiah and Alma. The situation appears to be quite different with Moroni; he seems to be uninfluenced in this way by the material he is editing.

It is obvious that much additional research on the authorship of the Book of Mormon can and will be conducted in the future as computer technology and scientific study advances. My purpose in discussing them here was not intended to be a complete and exhaustive review of what has been done, but rather to simply provide a greater understanding and appreciation of the unique word usages found in this ancient gold record.

Before sharing the final and, perhaps, the crowning experience in this treatise, I would like to step back for a moment and provide a perspective on human languages.

As illustrated in the chart below, the human languages are divided into several families. Our language, English, belongs to the Indo-European family. Central to this discussion is the Semitic family, comprised of five specific languages—Syrian, Hebrew, Ancient Egyptian, Arabic, and Aramaic. Of these, only Hebrew and Arabic remain upon the earth today. The other three are considered *dead* languages and are no longer in use. The Book of Mormon was originally written in "reformed Egyptian," as Moroni states in Mormon 9:32:

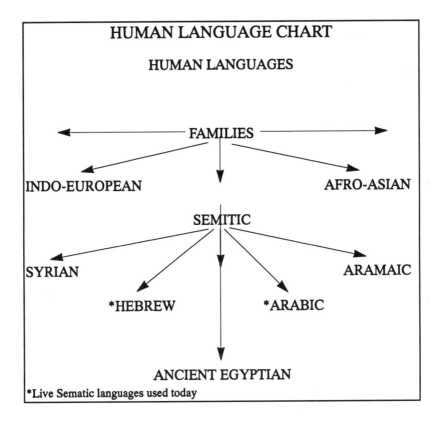

HUMAN LANGUAGE CHART

HUMAN LANGUAGES

FAMILIES

INDO-EUROPEAN   AFRO-ASIAN

SEMITIC

SYRIAN   ARAMAIC

*HEBREW   *ARABIC

ANCIENT EGYPTIAN

*Live Sematic languages used today

And now, behold, we have written this record according to our knowledge, in the characters which are called among us the reformed Egyptian, being handed down and altered by us, according to our manner of speech."

Father Lehi and his family spoke Hebrew as their first language, but because of the lengthy nature of the written Hebrew language, their *scribal*, or written, language was necessarily Egyptian. Egyptian was similar to our shorthand, in that much could be recorded on a given gold plate.

The original text came to us through Joseph Smith, being translated from the Semitic language that Moroni called "Reformed Egyptian," to the Indo-European language called "English."

Let us now come full circle to the events that unfolded in the early 1970's. At that time, our Church leaders determined that it would be a great blessing to translate the Book of Mormon back into its native Semitic tongue, thus providing this invaluable record for all those who read and spoke Hebrew and Arabic.

Because there are only *several hundred thousand people* who read and speak Hebrew, compared to the 800 million Moslems and Arabs who read and speak Arabic, the Brethren determined to first translate the book into Arabic.

It just so happened that teaching in the Department of Middle Eastern Studies at the University of Utah was a professor by the name of Sami Hanna. He was an Egyptian and was especially schooled in the Arabic language.

Dr. Hanna had transferred from the University of Chicago to accept this position in Utah, and had become intrigued with the Mormon culture in which he and his family found themselves. His interest was especially piqued when he found that Mormons credited their first prophet, Joseph Smith, with translating an ancient Egyptian record into English.

Events unfolded and Dr. Hanna ultimately accepted the assignment from the First Presidency to translate this same book (now a century and a half after the initial translation) back into its original Semitic cultural format. In his words:

> "When I began reading the Book of Mormon, and began making myself familiar with it, I expected to find a very poorly written book, as I had been told by critics of the unschooled nature of the youthful Joseph Smith as he had purportedly translated the book.
>
> What I found, however, was not a book of poor English; but to the contrary, I found myself reading the most beautiful Semitic book I had ever read! Naturally, it wasn't long before I knew that I must join the Church of Jesus Christ of Latter-day Saints. This I did, and I now hold the office of elder in the Church." (Taken from notes of the author at a Lecture by Dr. Sami Hanna March 18, 1975 to CES faculty in Salt Lake City, Utah.)

It was my privilege to sit at the feet of Dr. Hanna on two occasions for a total of eight hours. During that time, he unfolded one of the most fascinating journeys I have taken—delving deep into the pages of the Book of Mormon. He revealed a perspective that, until this time, had been known only to a limited number of Church scholars. At this time, I would like to take you on much the same journey as I have extrapolated from my frantic note-taking of the evenings spent with this gifted gentleman.

To begin with, Dr. Hanna pointed out that there are ten basic characteristics of the Semitic family of languages. Taken in context, these characteristics reveal Joseph Smith to be as he purported—a *translator*, not an author, of the Book of Mormon. They are as follows:

Semitic Characteristics of the Book of Mormon

Number One: Semitic writing is read from right to left.

The writing of the Indo-European culture is read from left to right. Joseph was informed of this characteristic when he first began to translate the plates.

Number Two: In the Semitic family of languages, there are no capital letters. One of the problems for each of the scribes during translation was in knowing just what words to capitalize. For example, Oliver Cowdery at one point wrote Jerusalem as "ger-Asulem." Many of the errors of the original manuscript involved capitalization. These scribes, or emenuenses, simply had no guide.

Number Three: There are no paragraphs in the Semitic languages.

In reviewing the original manuscript, very few paragraphs are inserted, which gave the printer, E.B. Grandin, a great deal of concern in typesetting the book.

Number Four: There is no punctuation in the Semitic languages. That culture simply does not use commas, periods, question marks, exclamation points, etc.

Of the nearly four thousand mistakes found in the original manuscript, most involved incorrect punctuation. In fact, Grandin was so concerned about this that he hired a young editor, John H. Gilbert, who spent several weeks editing the manuscript prior to typesetting, just so it would be readable. His task included adding punctuation, paragraphing, and most of the typesetting. Again, Joseph and his scribes had no real education to rely upon, so they simply did the best they could.

Number Five: In the Semitic languages, there are two verb tenses—past and present.

While we, in our culture, use a myriad of verb tenses such as past participle, Joseph became so knowledgeable in the Egyptian that he was able to restrict his verb usage to that of the Semitic culture.

Closely akin to this is the use of compound verbs such as "did go," "did eat," did smite," etc. While these verb forms are awkward and rarely used in English, they are classical, correct grammar in the Semitic languages.

Number Six: The use of function words in the published manuscript of the Book of Mormon is Semitic in nature. Three examples are as follows:

(1) In Helaman 3:14, there are a total of 18 "ands." Although the same number of "commas" have been inserted, the later editions of the book have kept all the "ands."

According to Dr. Hanna, each of these "ands" is necessary; the omission of any of them totally disallows meaning to the verse. Because no commas were initially inserted, each of these function words was necessary.

(2) In the 1830 edition of the Book of Mormon, we have the most pure repetition of the possessive pronoun, as provided in 1 Nephi 2:4, as follows:

And he left *his* house, and the land of *his* inheritance, and *his* gold, and *his* silver and *his* precious things. (italics added.)

The possessive pronoun "his" is necessary in all five parts of the sentence, just as the five "ands" are.

(3) The use of the cognate accusative, where the verb and the noun are matched, is purely Semitic. Three examples are "dreamed a dream," "work a work," and "write a writing."

Number Seven: The numbering system throughout the Book of Mormon is clearly Semitic. As illustrated in Helaman 3:36, there is a connective word "and" between each digit: "And it came to pass that the fifty *and* second year ended in peace."

If Joseph had been merely writing his own book, it would have been natural and expected for him to write "fifty-second year." But again, he was only translating from the hieroglyphics placed before him.

Number Eight: Proper nouns or names are semitic.

One of the most profound aspects of the 183 new names revealed in the Book of Mormon is that, without exception, they are of Semitic origin. Even to the disbeliever, it would seem an impossibility for the illiterate and youthful Joseph Smith to come forth with such a volume of new names in this period of time. That they correctly originate in the Semitic family becomes a compelling testimony of the book's origin.

The Semitic culture adds two additional vowels to the Indo-European, and so while many of the newly introduced names seem awkward for us to read, they are stunningly beautiful when expressed Semitically. An example Dr. Hanna presented was "Chemish." That name has always been difficult for me to say, but it comes alive with the proper vowels and pronunciation added.

Number Nine: The sentence structure is Semitic.

It stands to reason that a language is always spoken before it is written. In the Semitic culture, *suffixes* and *prefixes* are crucial to sentence development.

An example of this can be found in Enos 1:5. If Joseph were writing this himself, he would have written something like, "Enos, your sins are forgiven." Instead, he correctly translated "Enos, thy sins are forgiven *thee.*" This redundance seems awkward to us, but without the word "thee" at the end of this sentence, the entire sentence would be rendered meaningless in the Semitic culture.

Number Ten: Idioms used in the book are purely Semitic.

An *idiom* is an expression of thought that is peculiar to a given culture. Several Indo-European idioms are

For Pete's sake

Two bits

Holy cow

Lay an egg

Kick the bucket

Follow your nose

Hit the hay

Get the show on the road

Get the lead out

Perhaps the most recognizable Semitic characteristic in the translated Book of Mormon is the popular use of Semitic idioms. Several examples are as follows:

1. Alma 32:6—"And now when Alma heard this, he turned him[self] about." He didn't say turn "around," as we might say, but he turned *himself about.*

2. Alma 32:7—"But he stretched forth his hand." The Semitic culture uses body expressions and parts to portray action and feelings.

3. Alma 32:8—"I beheld that ye are lowly in heart." Again, they did not write simply "humble," as we might; they wrote, Semitically, "lowly in heart."

4. Words of Mormon 17—"and they did use much sharpness because of the *stiffneckedness* of the people." (italics added.) The word *stiffneckedness* is used many times throughout the Book of Mormon. If Joseph Smith had been writing his own book, he would likely have used "stubborn" or "inflexible." But in translating, he used the Semitic counterpart, the extremely awkward "stiffneckedness."

5. Alma 5:28—"Behold, are ye stripped of pride?" Again, a Semitic idiom.

6. Alma 5:37—"O ye workers of iniquity; ye that are puffed up in the vain things of the world." Both phrases, "workers of iniquity" and "puffed up," are Semitic expressions.

7. 1 Nephi 16:10—"And it came to pass that as my father arose in the morning, and went forth to the tent door, to his great astonishment he beheld upon the ground a round ball of *curious* workmanship." (italics added.) I had always related the word "curious" to "strange"; but according to Dr. Hanna, "curious" actually designates an instrument of "skilled" or "elegant" workmanship.

A second example of this word is found in 1 Nephi 18:1, as Nephi states, "And it came to pass that they did worship the Lord, and did go forth with me; and we did work timbers of curious workmanship." Again, these travelers became very skilled in their building of the ship in which they crossed the ocean, or "many waters."

Several more Semitic idioms found in the Book of Mormon are as follows:

8. "Fountains" means "springs and streams."

9. "Many waters" means "oceans," as illustrated in 1 Nephi 13:10, 12-13, 29.

10. "Turned aside their ears" means "forsook the Lord."

11. "Face of the land" means "terrain."

12. "Four quarters of the earth" means "everywhere."

13. "By the hand of" means "written by."

14. "By the mouth of" means "spoken by."

15. "Reigned in his stead" means "presided after someone else."

16. "Having dwelt" means "came from."

17. "Plates of Brass" not "Brass Plates."

18. "Spoken by the mouth of" instead of "said."

In addition to the above, Dr. Hanna provided several specific Semitic statements as follows:

1. In Alma 63:11, reference is made to Helaman, the son of Helaman. This would have been an unnatural term for Joseph, who referred to himself as "Joseph Smith, Jun." throughout his lifetime. In the Semitic culture, however, there is no word for "Junior." Instead, a person with the same name as his father is called "the son of."

2. In the Semitic culture, a 30-day period is called a "moon" rather than a "month." Even though Joseph uses "month" a couple of times in his translation (thus giving credence to his humanness in quickly working through each plate), primarily he gives this time period the Semitic "moon" identity.

3. In Omni 18, Lehi's great-great-grandson, Omni, states: "Zarahemla gave a genealogy of his fathers, according to his memory." As Dr. Hanna states, it is a very typical custom of his Semitic forbearers to recite their genealogy from their memory, thus passing it down from one generation to another.

4. In Mosiah 11:8 we read: "King Noah built many elegant and spacious buildings; and he ornamented them with fine work of wood . . . and precious things," including "*ziff.*" (italics added.)

The word "ziff" is not contained in the English language; yet Dr. Hanna states that in Arabic it means "a special kind of curved sword, somewhat like a scimitar, which is carried in a sheath and is often used for ornamentation as well as for fighting."

5. In Helaman 1:3, reference is made to three brothers contending for the judgment-seat. Joseph, rather than using the terms "senate," "president," or "ruler," used the Semitic phrase, "judgment-seat."

Dr. Hanna affirms that in Arabic custom, the place of power rests in the judgment-seat, and that whoever occupies that seat is the authority. He emphasizes that the authority goes with the seat, not with the office or the person. Thus, a perfect Semitic phrase!

6. In Ether 2:17, we learn that the Jaredites built their barges under the direction of the Lord, and that "the length therefore was the length of a tree." In the Semitic culture, common objects are used to relate distances, etc. Therefore, this phrase is completely within Semitic context.

Though this discussion could continue, hopefully it has served to provide a new lens through which you can now view this ancient Semitic journal. As Dr. Hanna stated, upon first reading the Book of Mormon, there is truly no way that even a learned Indo-European man of today could produce such a perfectly Semitic book. When we consider that in 1829 a twenty-three-year-old man with a formal education of merely three years, produced this book, our minds are profoundly subdued. When we also consider that Joseph completed this task in just sixty days, some of the actual translating, amidst persecution, moving, receiving revelations, caring for his family, etc., we begin to glimpse the near superhuman nature of his work.

But work, Joseph did. He utilized two instruments of interpretation, as well as several scribes. In the end, he produced what he later called "the most correct book upon the face of the earth."

Part Four

For the present, we conclude our travels. Still, I have meant our journeys to be merely treks of preparation; for the real climb must be our daily, faith-filled walk into the pages of this unique canon of scripture.

President Ezra Taft Benson has stated the Book of Mormon has three purposes: first, to serve as the "keystone" of our religion; second, to serve as a record that was written for our day; and third, to provide us with a vehicle in which we can move closer to our Maker and his Son.

Perhaps I could at this time share one example of the second purpose, which actually leads into the third.

As we begin reading the Book of Mosiah, we find ourselves enjoying an ancient general conference of the Church, held about 124 B.C. King Benjamin was the spiritual head of his people and delivered a farewell address to them. This address, from my perspective, is second in power and in content only to the Savior's Sermon on the Mount. It contains so much meat that I still am not able to digest it all. I have tried, even to the extent of reading the entire address almost every morning for several successive weeks, but still there are new insights to gain.

We are told in Mosiah that King Benjamin was visited by an angel, and that he was schooled in what to tell his people; so the comprehensive and timely nature of his message to his people (as well as to us, in our day) is even more compelling. From Mosiah 4:14-15, I quote:

And ye will not suffer your children that they go hungry, or naked; neither will ye suffer that they transgress the laws of God, and fight and quarrel one with another, and serve the devil, who is the master of sin, or who is the evil spirit which hath been spoken of by our fathers, he being an enemy to all righteousness. "But ye will teach them to walk in the ways of truth and soberness; ye will teach them to love one another, and to serve one another.

Not long ago, I shared this scripture with my wife, Margaret, and she immediately keyed in on the final phrase, "teach them to love one another, and to serve one another." She then determined to try out this formula of loving by serving.

Later that afternoon, when our fifteen-year-old son, Jeremy, came into the kitchen, she asked, "Jeremy, will you please clean up the kitchen?"

His reply was anticipated, "Why me, Mom? Why do I have to do it?"

"Because I need you to love me more, Jeremy; and if you do something for me, you will love me."

Uncomplaining, Jeremy quickly completed the task. Then, hurrying to play a basketball game at the church, he kissed his mother good-bye and told her how much he loved her.

The impressive observation for us is how Jeremy and the rest of our children have come to appreciate that they truly love those they serve. Serving one another in the home is the perfect way to increase the level of love we feel for those in our homes.

This is but one example of numberless applications our family has made of the writings of these early American prophets. The point I want to make is that when we are reading the Book of Mormon each day, we can receive prescriptions for our own lives. These applications from the Book of Mormon will come as dew from heaven, as promised to Joseph while he was in the Liberty Jail (D&C 121).

The final and, of course *central* purpose of the Book of Mormon is to teach us of Christ, him crucified and resurrected. There are moments in my life when I seriously question how earnestly we, as a people, are seeking to know and understand the Savior and his plan. It is so easy to smugly pass out personalized copies of the Book of Mormon and then to neglect to learn for ourselves and for our children the process of becoming like him, as taught within the pages of that sacred, holy record.

Elder Bruce R. McConkie, in his book *The Promised Messiah*, includes a poignant chapter titled "Seek The Face of the Lord Always." Within this chapter, on page 571, he states:

> There are two applications to be made of the great and eternal truths concerning the Promised Messiah. As believing saints it is our privilege:
>
> 1. To enjoy the gift of the Holy Ghost; to receive personal revelation; to possess the signs that always follow true believers; to work miracles; and to have the gifts of the Spirit; and
>
> 2. To see the Lord face to face; to talk with him as a man speaketh with his friend; to have his Person attend us from time to time; and to have him manifest to us the Father.

From my limited, though striving perspective, the great blessing and power of the Book of Mormon is that, more than any other book, it teaches us how to learn of the One who is to become our Friend. We become Christ's friend as we meet him face to face. And now, in solemn preparation, we are able to learn of him from a pure and undefiled journal—the Book of Mormon.

I am caused to reflect upon what my wife's visiting teaching companion, Mary Lee Lake, shared recently regarding her experience with the Book of Mormon. She said, and I quote, "Reading the Book of Mormon, for me, is like painting the Golden Gate Bridge. Once I finish it, I must begin at once to read it again so the ideas in it don't become rusty. I am truly never finished with this marvelous scripture."

President Benson has said that if we read and study this book, we naturally draw near to God, and we have greater power when we are involved in it. In putting the lengthy discussion of these pages in perspective, I would like to quote his words, as recorded in the Conference Report, April, 1987, *Ensign*, May 1987, pp. 83-84.

> We are not required to prove that the Book of Mormon is true or is an authentic record through external evidences—though there are many. It never has been the case, nor is it so now, that the studies of the learned will prove the Book of Mormon true or false. The origin, preparation, translation, and verification of the truth of the Book of Mormon have all been retained in the hands of the Lord, and the Lord makes no mistakes. You can be assured of that.

God has built his own proof system of the Book of Mormon as found in Moroni, chapter 10, and in the testimonies of the Three and the Eight Witnesses [as well as] in various sections of the Doctrine and Covenants. We each need to get our own testimony of the Book of Mormon through the Holy Ghost. Then our testimony, coupled with the Book of Mormon, should be shared with others so that they, too, can know through the Holy Ghost of its truthfulness.

It is my sincere hope that we will build up faith in this prophetic journal that was written for our day, and that we will do as Moroni directed—that is, read it *with a sincere heart, with real intent, having faith in Christ.* A testimony of faith, after all, is much more valuable than a testimony of knowledge. In fact, from my experience, a testimony of knowledge must become a supportive testimony to that of faith.

Hopefully, this writing has been more than an intellectual exercise. I hope that it has provided meat to consider and perspective to draw upon, as we continue to refine our spiritual faculties. If we are successful in this, we will ultimately prepare ourselves *and* our families to meet our Savior—the final author of this unique book—and thus become his adopted children as well as his true friends.

About the Author

Born and reared in central Utah, Brenton G. Yorgason served an LDS mission to Florida and Puerto Rico, was set apart as a special missionary while stationed in the Army in Viet Nam, and later received a Ph.D. from Brigham Young University, majoring in Family Studies, and minoring in Marriage and Family Therapy.

Brenton is author or coauthor of over forty books, with total sales of well over one million copies. In additon to writing, Brenton is a practicing marriage and family therapist. He is also a nationally recognized corporate 'Keynote' speaker and a member of the National Speaker's Association.

Brenton and his wife, Margaret, are the parents of seven sons and two daughters and reside in Sandy, Utah.